Test Your Toddler's IQ

RACHEL FEDERMAN
ILLUSTRATIONS BY
ELLEN T. CRENSHAW

Skyhorse Publishing

For Wally—my now-out-of-toddler-hood little advisor who taught me how to be tested by a toddler daily

DISCLAIMER: This is a book of humor. Caution should be used in all activities, and safety and responsibility rest with the reader. The author and publisher do not accept responsibility for injury or damage.

Contents

Introduction

You made it to the first birthday party, and we know *you* blew out the candles only because your one-year-old was too busy practicing clarinet—not because you were really celebrating *your* first year as a parent. Congratulations are in order! You've now mastered co-sleeping or sleep training or musical beds or the art of enduring hours of howling and tears at bedtime (mostly your own). You've puréed a million organic veggies, shampooed hairless heads, and developed an incredibly high tolerance for all kinds of smells and unidentified piles of goop. You've learned to keep Tabasco sauce out of reach and how to treat paper cuts you got shuffling through endless baby sign language flash cards. You've strolled, you've swung, you've swaddled, you've slung, and you've showered friends with hourly photo updates only grandparents should be made to endure. Now you're ready for things to get much easier—or much harder, depending on whose advice sounds most convincing at any given moment.

Now your little one wanders more and sleeps less. He cries fewer hours but with much greater force each time. Your complaints about round-the-clock feedings have turned into grumbles about picky eating. Forget swaddling and sterilizing, and most everything else you needed to know the first year. There's a whole new set of rules now, and we hope you're ready for the chase! And not just chasing your toddler around the apartment and the playground and the grocery store and the backyard, but chasing all those super-advanced prodigy toddlers in the neighborhood who might, right this very minute, be getting ahead of yours.

Now that you've had a few seconds to look back on your accomplishments this past year, we know you're ready to move forward and answer that most pressing of questions: *Is your toddler an undiscovered genius?*

Except you know the answer to that already: Yes. What you really want to know is what *type* of genius. In the questions that follow we're going to take a look at your toddler in various settings—on a neighborhood walk or at a museum, for example—to narrow down her particular strengths. Would she rather spend the day surrounded by books or hopping along a bubbling brook? Does she seek out sensory experiences, scientific experiments, or the chance to muse about her place in the universe? For most questions, try to remember your toddler in a similar situation, or make your best guess as to what you think your little guy or gal would likely do in the circumstances. Find out what makes your toddler tick, what makes him trip, and whether he'll likely grow up to be a Scientist, Philosopher, Creator/Entertainer, Entrepreneur, or Explorer.

In the Activity Exam you'll set up trials to "test" your child's behavior. Please supervise him at all times and use your best judgment about what kinds of activities are appropriate. Although the book's title makes it sound like a race to crown the most advanced toddler, in reality we just want to help you find out a little bit more about your wonder child. If she's learning to crawl while a neighbor's tot is dancing the jitterbug, remember the story about the tortoise and the hare. (And keep in mind that legend has it Albert Einstein didn't start speaking until he was four.)

Maybe your wunderkind offspring's test results won't win you the parent-of-the-smartest-kid-in-town award. She may never come up with a theory to rival Einstein's one about relativity. Heck, maybe she'll never even impress relatives with a recitation of the times tables at a holiday dinner. But once you manage to string together a few hours of uninterrupted sleep, you'll realize that every year you get to spend together is its own miracle.

Chapter One

Every Day with Your Toddler

Life with a toddler. What could be more fun? Or more tiring? Or messier? Or require more patience and endurance? Or serve as a better test of your character? But we're getting ahead of ourselves, just as a toddler does the minute they learn to walk, especially in crowded, dangerous places. More on that later; for now, we're testing your toddler, not you. Let's get a general sense of who he or she actually is.

1. Which question is your toddler most likely to ask?

A How many times do you think this bee's wings flap per second?

B Do humans have free will?

C Can I finger paint today?

D Do you think anyone would buy my old chew toys?

E What's on the other side of that playground?

2. When is your toddler happiest?

A When she has unlimited access to blocks

B When she has unlimited access to books

C When she performs *Frozen* songs at family holidays

D When she's playing ice cream shop

E When we go on a family hike

3. When is your toddler the quietest?

A When he's concentrating on a puzzle

B When he's meditating

C When he's drawing on the newly painted walls

D When you're on an important work call (naturally, he wants to be conferenced in)

E You have obviously never met my toddler

4. Which activity takes the longest to complete?

A Clearing up his Periodic Table of the Elements blocks

B Attempting to reconcile Plato's theory of forms with Heidegger's more controversial claims about the afterlife

C Perfecting an arabesque

D Working out a sippy cup budget

E Sketching out the route for that day's hike

5. Which activity are you able to get done with your toddler by your side?

A Releasing mice caught in humane traps

B Dusting the furniture

C Decorating the table for a dinner party

D Promoting my latest business idea

E Looking for a new apartment

TIP: Once you have kids, any chores at all—even grocery shopping at rush hour or cleaning the bathroom—when performed in solitude, magically transform into the most indulgent of leisurely "me-time" activities!

Chapter Two

Playtime

In the same way that playtime for babies isn't just about playing any more, the same is true for toddlers. They're learning all kinds of things about their surroundings and themselves when they toss a ball back and forth or dress a doll, not least that they're not the center of the world. Let's find out a little bit about how your toddler likes to spend his free time.

1. Who does your toddler most often pretend to be?

 Charles Darwin

B Aristotle

 Claude Monet

D Bill Gates

E Ernest Shackleton

2. Which toy would your child like the best?

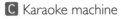 **A** Magnifying glass

B Stone

C Karaoke machine

D Lemonade stand

E Binoculars

3. What is your toddler's favorite thing to do with a piece of paper?

A Make a paper airplane

B Draft a rebuttal to Descartes

C Rip it up into tiny pieces and throw confetti

D Make a to-do list

E Ball it up and throw it at me

4. Which scenario best describes the fort-building process in your home?

A It's hard to drag her away from the latest issue of the *Journal of Cell Biology* long enough to find out

B I build a fort while my toddler quietly observes

C We work together, as I try not to freak out about all the sheets and blankets and towels I will have to wash

D My toddler works on getting a patent for his structurally sound, load-bearing pillow roof

E I build a fort while my toddler crashes into it and tears it down

5. When you sing "Head, Shoulders, Knees, and Toes," which part does your toddler excel at?

A Pointing to the correct body parts (even when going double time)

B Endurance (stays engaged for at least five rounds)

C Singing on key

D Leading everybody else in the song

E Inventing new verses

6. What is your toddler most likely to do with a crayon?

A Ask you what temperature it melts at

B Posit the difference between teal and aqua

C Use it as a person in a dollhouse

D Write her name

E Take a bite (Please just speculate about this one! Don't actually try it.)

7. What does it mean if your toddler is happily occupying himself for way too long?

A He's figured out the passcode to my iPad

B He's found the opening of *Jude the Obscure* much more compelling than you did

C He's figured out a way to tie-dye my brand-new white sundress

D He's convincing an older child to break into the cookie jar

E He's plotting an escape route

8. What is your toddler's favorite art supply?

A Paper-making kit

B Water paint

C Mezzo-fresco

D Poster paint

E Whatever we're having for dinner that night

9. Which TV show does your toddler like best?

 A Sid the Science Kid

B Cosmos

C American Idol

D Shark Tank

E Dora the Explorer

10. When you play follow-the-leader, what does the game most closely resemble?

A A chemistry lab

B An attempt to prove your existence

C A dance class

D A strategy session

E A walk on the moon

Chapter Three

Mealtime

That dreaded time of day that pops up with such regularity! Of all the advice people are most desperate to heap on new parents, pointers about mealtimes probably top the list. Some people will tell you to withhold dessert until plates are licked clean. Others will say you should never offer dessert as a reward. Some say let the kids pick and choose what they want. The French typically caution against catering to a child's tastes, recommending instead that you serve something healthy that adults like and let them adapt. I've found that kids eat best when they're focused on least (when company is over, wine is flowing, and no one's buying tickets to their "What is this unholy poison?!" show). How do mealtimes work at your house?

1. Which would be your toddler's favorite dinner?

A Bread sticks twisted into the shape of a DNA strand

B Blended organic veggies

C An "I give up" meal (i.e., some combination of chicken nuggets, French fries, hot dogs, and mac 'n' cheese)

D The taco pizza he invented

E Anything with a foreign name and a ginger glaze, herb crust, and balsamic reduction

2. Does your toddler prefer:

A To be spoon fed with airplane sounds?

B To be spoon fed without fanfare?

C Finger food (if she's old enough)?

D Doubling mealtimes with brainstorming sessions?

E Packing up a picnic lunch?

3. Which mealtime present do you get the most use out of?

A The squirt spoon

B The good china

C The Picasso bowl

D The "I'm the boss" sippy cup

E A map of the U.S.A. placemat

4. If you ask your toddler for a little bit of what she's eating, does she:

A Happily share, letting you help yourself?

B Feed you?

C Grudgingly let you take a bite?

D Trade you a bite?

E Shake her head and make the classic toddler angry face?

5. What is the fanciest restaurant to which you can take your toddler (without fear of a major meltdown)?

A Pizza joint

B Gozen Sushi

C The preschool cafeteria

D The Four Seasons

E We're still working on French fries at the playground without a major meltdown

Chapter Four

Outdoors

Even the fastest-moving toddler slows to a screeching halt whenever you take him for a walk and attempt to actually get somewhere. But if there's nowhere you have to get to, and no time constraints, you'll have the best time. Toddlers are spontaneous, close observers of nature, and extremely tolerant of long detours and repeated delays (especially if they involve mud or puddles, preferably both). A one-year-old will treat the most pedestrian sight as a great wonder of the world, and will find pigeons, fences—even shiny pieces of trash—objects of endless fascination. Let's find out how your toddler navigates the great outdoors, or even just a sidewalk in the 'burbs.

1. What's the easiest way to take your toddler for a walk?

A Set her free, and be sure to bring a notebook to jot down your observations

B Strap her into a carrier

C A combination of picking her up, putting her down, picking her up, putting her down…

D In the stroller

E Try to walk hand-in-hand (with a lot more chasing than you'd ideally like)

2. If you take the stroller, which of the following scenarios is most likely?

A He whines and bucks around, begging to be let out

B He stays happily buckled in, enjoying the scenery but wondering how to prove a shared reality

C We end up both walking, pushing along the empty stroller

D I end up in the stroller while he pushes

E He turns the stroller into a spaceship

3. How does your toddler react to a friendly neighbor waving hi?

 By measuring her velocity

B By asking her about the nature of time

C By giving an impromptu performance of "Hello" by Adele

D By asking how her day has been going so far

E By screaming, "Get away! Get away, mean lady!"

4. Which of the following is most likely to catch his attention?

A A construction site

B A drop of dew

C Another toddler

D An empty lot

E Anything he's not allowed to touch

5. How does your toddler react to the sight of harmless bugs?

A She's only interested in insect metamorphosis—particularly the pupal stage

B She gains perspective about her role in the life cycle

C She sings a song for them

D She likes me to take pictures of them

E She begs to take them home

6. If your toddler brings a toy outside, what are the chances that he will lose it?

A He might lose it, but he'll easily build a new one from fabric scraps and pom-poms

B He'll lose part of it, but come home with its essence

C He would never risk it

D He'll come home with a completely different toy, and I'll have no idea how that happened

E Almost 100%

7. Which of the following natural places do you think your little one is most likely to explore when she gets a bit older?

A A forest

B A beach

C A mountain

D Whatever looks best posted on social media

E Mars

8. When outside, what sounds are most attractive to your toddler?

A Bird calls

B Someone reading Nietzsche aloud

C Her own voice

D The ice cream truck

E The sound of a tree falling in the forest

9. On a nature walk, is your toddler happiest when:

A Pointing out a butterfly to you?

B Listening to you tell him about the seasons?

C Heading home?

D Complaining about the weather?

E Discovering a new path?

10. What is the most likely reason you'll turn around and go home?

A She needs to refer to something in her botany handbook

B She wants to figure out if she can "be here now," wherever she is

C She wants to draw a picture of a blossoming tree

D She owes someone money and doesn't want to chance a run-in

E She needs to gather more supplies

Chapter Five

Other People

Who says having a whiny, half-naked, totally irrational human being in your house means you can't go out in public? After all, there is still an entire real world out there, one that exists beyond your child's Instagrammable milestones. There are, in fact, all kinds of people ready to judge your every parenting move. Because your stroller is full of Cheerios crumbs. Or because you're wearing the same shirt as yesterday (and the day before). Or because you have an unexplained stain the shape of Louisiana on your cheek. Or because you gave in to your toddler's whines and let him eat your chocolate croissant. Or because you *ignored* your toddler's whines and didn't let him eat said chocolate croissant. Be prepared not only for superior glares and under-the-breath critiques, but for constant advice about everything you're doing wrong. From strangers. Let's find out how your toddler (and you) fare on these rejuvenating outings.

1. What kind of expedition is generally the most fun with your toddler? (Using the term "fun" very loosely and making an immediate note to get your hands on Jennifer Senior's book *All Joy and No Fun: The Paradox of Modern Parenting*.)

A A natural history museum

B Taking a quiet walk in the park and maybe even going off-grid

C Breakdancing for strangers in a crowded playground

D A visit to the local Mommy (or Daddy) and Me Start-up group

E The zoo (we're not the loudest ones!)

2. At library storytime, which description best matches your little cutie?

A Remembers all the hand motions to "Itsy Bitsy Spider"

B Sits shyly on your lap and refuses to participate

C Reads the story

D Conducts his own research in the business and finance section

E Pulls the fire alarm

3. At Mommy (or Daddy) and Me Yoga class, your toddler is most likely to:

A Find a correlation between age and flexibility of participants

B Achieve an enlightened meditative state

C Demonstrate the tortoise pose for the class

D Try to cheer up the boy who has been screaming since the lotus position

E Dig through your purse and find something to destroy

4. You take your toddler to a dentist appointment and forget to bring a toy.

Does she:

A Hand the dentist the tongue retractor?

B Wait patiently in the chair?

C Dance to entertain you, making it hard not to laugh despite the Novocain?

D Make a sculpture with cotton balls and tape?

E Dig through your purse, draw with your lipstick, and accidentally butt-call your boss?

5. You bravely attempt an enriching outing to the art museum. Things go well for an entire ten minutes while you visit the snack bar, but then take the inevitable downward turn when your toddler:

A Hurls himself over the rope marking off a traveling Rembrandt

B Stages a meltdown because he doesn't like umbrellas on a sunny day in a Georges Seurat painting

C Treats other visitors to a live demonstration of Edvard Munch's *The Scream*

D Shows only the faintest interest in the new addition to the 19th-century wing

E I would never even dream of bringing him any place where you are not encouraged to full body smash Every. Single. Thing.

6. Would other parents describe you as a:

A Helicopter parent?

B Friend parent?

C 1950s "Go run along now" parent?

D Tiger parent?

E Free-range parent?

7. Which book would someone most likely buy you after observing you for an hour out and about?

A *The Three-Martini Playdate* by Christie Mellor

B *The Blessing of a Skinned Knee* by Wendy Mogel

C *The Idle Parent* by Tom Hodgkinson

D *No Regrets Parenting* by Harley A. Rotbart, M.D.

E *NurtureShock* by Po Bronson and Ashley Merryman

8. Which member of your community hates you the most now that you have kids?

A Upstairs neighbor (they still haven't gotten over the cry-it-out method)

B Your deliveryman (Mama needs her midnight ramen)

C Downstairs neighbor (too much toddler gymnastics + high-heel dress up = not a great combo)

D Your boss

E Your friends ("What do you mean you don't want to dance on a bar and do pickle-back shots until 3 A.M. anymore?")

9. You take your child to a friend's outdoor concert. What is your pride and joy most likely to do?

A Ask about the sound system

B Become one with the music

C Beg to rush home so he can write his own song

D Set up a booth to sell the crackers you brought

E Whine until you agree to leave the concert and explore the nearby wildlife refuge

10. What is the worst thing your child is likely to do at a dinner party?

A Take an overly rigid stance on immigration

B Forget to say thank you

C Say, "Look, Mommy, they have your favorite kind of coffee," pointing to a bottle of Pinot Grigio

D Comment that the French onion soup had a hint too much lemon

E Break an antique mirror

Chapter Six

Bedtime

Bedtime is many parents' favorite time of the day—right up there with naptime. But the lead-up to bedtime can be so draining and intense that we often put it off rather than wrestle the little sprites into their beds so they can have sweet dreams while we binge-watch entire seasons of our latest addiction.

Parents know that the minute you grab your snacks and remote control and snuggle under a cozy blanket … Wait for it. A padding of little feet down the hall. A high voice—and there they are! They're back up again. Repeat your tucking-in routine many, many times, until you finally give up on your much-deserved, much-delayed, much-deferred precious "me time" and go to bed yourself. That is bedtime with a toddler. Let's track your toddler's bedtime behavior to round out the picture of your offspring's potent potential.

1. At the end of a long day, which reward would your child pick for good behavior?

A A trip to the local observatory

B Extra dessert

C Baking a gluten-free Tiramisu cake with you

D Picking out a new toy

E Staying outside after sunset

2. Which book does your toddler enjoy the most before bed?

A *A Brief History of Time* by Stephen Hawking

B *The Cat in the Hat* by Dr. Seuss

C *Pinkalicious* by Victoria Kann and Elizabeth Kann

D *Sheep in a Jeep* by Nancy Shaw

E *The 7 Worst Things Good Parents Do* by John C. Friel, Ph.D., and Linda D. Friel, M.A.

3. Which activity would your toddler find most relaxing?

A Dissecting a frog

B Climbing a tree

C Working on her stand-up routine

D Meeting with key investors

E Finding the world's best hiding spot

4. Where would your sleepyhead most want to sleep?

A Anywhere in the visible universe

B In the present moment

C At a hotel in the Theater District

D Under his desk

E Under the stars

5. After the usual nighttime routine—bath, teeth, potty, "nothing's coming," pull-up, peed-in-pull-up-and-need-a-new-one, can't find favorite stuffed bear, will die if cannot find (different one from last night), last sip of water, night light on, curtains closed, lullaby sung three times—what sound is most likely to come from your toddler's room?

A Snoring

B "Do you believe in lucid dreaming?"

C Something reminiscent of early Van Halen

D "If you read *Pajama Time!* just once more, I'll make my bed in the morning"

E A request for more potable water, preferably in a canteen

Activity Exam

The following questions ask you to conduct trials with your toddler. Please use your best judgment to adapt the suggestions based on your child's particular skills and development. If anything sounds like it might be uncomfortable or problematic in any way, please skip it. This section is meant to be fun—a chance for you to examine your toddler's behavior in more detail and hopefully enjoy the time together.

Check out page 124 for some suggested Brain Boosters, if you want to stack the deck before beginning!

1. Show your toddler that you are hiding a toy, but ask him to look away as you hide it. Pick a place that is hidden from view but not too difficult (i.e., behind a couch pillow).

Set your timer. How long does it take him to find it?

A Hasn't found it yet, but we located the missing hard-boiled Easter egg from last year

B Hasn't found it yet; he's more interested in establishing the toy's existence

C 2–5 minutes

D Over 5 minutes

E He's found another toy

94

2. Ask your toddler what he sees in the picture. Which of the answers below is closest to the one he gives?

A A giraffe

B An ink blot

C Mick Jagger

D An iMac

E French toast

3. Cut out a magazine picture that corresponds to an item around the house (a couch or a plant, for example). Show your toddler the picture and ask him to find the actual object. Does he:

A Take you to the corresponding item in the house?

B Point to the picture?

C Tell you that the picture of the couch is way nicer than your actual couch?

D Tell you he's busy but he'll be in touch soon?

E Attempt to repair the ripped page with tape?

4. Give your toddler a pair of your matching socks, separated. Does she:

A Put them on herself?

B Attempt to put them on you?

C Ball them together?

D Put them away in the drawer?

E Use them as hand puppets?

BONUS QUESTION:

If you ball the socks together and throw them into an empty bucket, how likely is your toddler to understand the game and join in?

A She'll join, unless you let her try another volcano experiment with baking soda and vinegar

B She's too distracted by the cat

C You're still searching for a pair of matching socks

D Your request is met with an unexplained, sudden toddler wail and drop to the floor

E She can free-throw from center court

5. Pick up a toy and look your toddler in the eye. Then ask in a light, sing-songy voice, "Do you want to play with me?" Your toddler:

A Grabs the toy out of your hand and wails?

B Says "Yes," but immediately becomes distracted by someone cooler than you?

C Babbles something cheerful but incoherent?

D Questions the sincerity of your tone?

E Uses the toy to hit the glass coffee table like a drum?

6. Blow bubbles for your toddler (please don't blow them directly into his face, and make sure he doesn't swallow the solution). Does he:

A Read the ingredients to make sure none of them are toxic?

B Attempt to capture the bubbles, but mostly end up popping them while ruminating on the nature of transience?

C Try to grab the wand so he can blow?

D Encourage you to wave the wand rather than blow for higher productivity?

E Pop the bubbles on purpose?

7. Play a shell game with your toddler by putting a cracker (or any other kind of snack you deem safe) under one of three plastic cups. To warm up, have your toddler point to the cup where the snack is hiding. Then move the cups around and ask your toddler where it is. Does she:

A Point to the correct cup?

B Point to the wrong cup?

C Get a drink of water with one of the cups?

D Build a sales office with the cups?

E Suggest you take the shell game on the road and offer to be your accomplice?

8. Give your baby a small stuffed animal. When he is holding one, offer him another. Does he:

A Let go of the first to take the second?

B Hold one in each hand?

C Try to hold two in one hand but end up dropping one?

D Hand the first one back to you?

E Juggle?

9. Hide your face behind a pillow and say, "Where's Mommy (or Daddy)?" Which of the following best describes how your little one reacts?

A She says (in a no-nonsense voice): "You're right here. I can see the rest of your body"

B She answers with a question, "Who can say?"

C She giggles and repeats, "Where's Mommy?"

D She removes the pillow and says you're going to need a better gimmick

E She comes around to your side of the pillow and hides with you

10. Give your toddler the following four-step verbal sequence:

1. Sit down.

2. Clap your hands.

3. Bark like a dog.

4. Close your eyes.

How many of the steps does he get through?

A All of them

B 1–3

C He completes them in backward order

D He asks for written instructions

E I lost him at "Sit down"

11. Show your child the next page and ask, "Which face is happy? Show me." What does she do?

A She points to the happy face

B She points to one of the other faces

C She makes a happy face

D She attempts to draw her own happy face

E She didn't slow down long enough to see the faces

12. Ask your child, "Which face doesn't want to leave the playground when his mom says it's time to go?"

A He points to the angry or sad face

B He points to one of the other faces

C He asks to go to the playground

D He gives you a bored, slightly amused look

E He takes a marker and crosses all the faces out

109

13. Teach your toddler the sign language for "more" and ask her to repeat it. Check all that apply.

A She repeats the sign once and asks to learn something else in sign language

B She repeats the sign and then goes off to do something else

C She incorporates the sign into a pretty rockin' song and dance number

D She incorporates the sign into a slogan

E She uses the sign to ask for a second helping of kale at dinner that night

14. Ask your child to walk like a gorilla. Does she:

A Pound her chest and say "thump, thump" as she walks?

B Walk like a dog?

C Walk like an Egyptian?

D Ask what you'll do for her?

E Grab her binoculars and look around for the nearest herbivorous ape?

15. Read the short William Carlos Williams poem "This Is Just to Say" out loud. Which answer best describes your toddler's reaction?

A He runs to the refrigerator to look for plums

B He continues pushing his train along an invisible track, appearing lost in thought about what the poem says about the possibility for redemption

C He counters with his own poem, swapping in bananas for plums, unconcerned about the irregularity of the resulting rhythm

D He thinks you paid too much for plums

E He plans a plum-picking expedition for late May

16. Hand your child a copy of Marcel Proust's *Remembrance of Things Past* (or some other tome). Does she:

A Open it and read upside down?

B Open it and read right-side up?

C Use it as a block in the castle she's building?

D Use the return of it as a bargaining chip for extra dessert that night?

E Use it as a stepstool to reach the bag of cookies you stashed away?

17. Play Mozart's *Eine kleine Nachtmusik* while your toddler is engaged in another activity. Does he:

A Refer to the piece by its official title ("Serenade No. 13 in G Major") and ask who conducted the version you're playing?

B Listen as if in a trance, staring out the window?

C Grab his kazoo and play along?

D Ask about the limits to copyright claims for jingles?

E Ask about the potential connection to the musical by Stephen Sondheim?

18. Play red light, green light with your little engine, and call out "Red light." Does he:

A Slow down gradually, making it clear his heart isn't in the game?

B Stop immediately, and so gracefully you wonder if he ever moved?

C Ask you to sing the commands?

D Insist he get to shout out "Red light/Green light," and never relinquish his position of power?

E Tell you he'd love to play another day, but right now he's got somewhere else he needs to be?

Analyzing Your Tot's Score

Mostly As—Scientist/Scholar
There's no toy your tot doesn't want to take apart, no shell he doesn't want to take home for his collection, no question about outer space that doesn't take his breath away. He'd rather understand the mechanics of your iPhone than talk on it or play *Minecraft*. He's more curious about how water interacts with paint than what kind of picture he can create. He may be shy in certain settings, and it's possible he missed a lesson or two about etiquette while reading up on the physical properties of molecules, but let your little questioner follow his inquiring mind and he'll go far.

Mostly Bs—Philosopher
She may be little, but she sees the big picture, and she'll help you step back from the daily frustrations that can sometimes obscure your view. She doesn't need grand adventure to satisfy her because no matter where she is—at the local playground, sitting at the table, or lying on the couch—her mind is focused on trying to grasp time, reality, ethics, and her place in the universe. Sure, she might be a little pale, and not

just because she always remembers her zinc oxide sunscreen, but she's soaking up knowledge like a sponge. She'll be happy with a pile of books, a trip to the library, and a chance to dig deeper (as long as the digging is metaphorical).

Appreciate her endless insight and enlightened state, but make sure that while she's keeping herself in the moment, she's enjoying it, too. Sometimes a swing is just a swing, and it's great fun to take a ride on it.

Mostly Cs—Creator/Entertainer

She loves to soak up art, music, and culture, but is happiest fashioning her own interpretation of the world. She thinks of a twist to any game you suggest, swoons at de Kooning, and listens with rapt attention when you read out loud. You may be annoyed by her attention-getting antics at times, but you'll never be bored around your little showstopper. She's been bopping her head to music from the moment she could hold up her neck, and she's never happier than when all eyes are on her. She's also content to spend the day inside with finger paints and glitter glue—and of course doesn't confine her work to paper, but considers the walls, chairs, and your first edition signed copy of *The World According to Garp* fair game. This is, after all, the world according to her.

Her love of the spotlight also means she'll often impress with advanced social skills—she's aware of the positive reaction she gets and seeks it out—but it also means she can be overly concerned with what others think. Get her to rely on her own validation when she's older, but for now just enjoy the show.

Mostly Ds—Entrepreneur

Your headstrong little exec is the one calling the shots and thinking of new ideas faster than you can say, "Ready. Set. Go."

He has a knack for seeing the opportunity in every situation, and will jump at the chance to garner some venture capital, especially in the form of Goldfish or cheese sticks. Sometimes his headstrong nature means he wants to go his own way, but whenever he starts up with you, just think about his potential for starting up his own business one day! He likely has great ideas on how to maximize your daily productivity, but make sure he knows that time isn't really money; once basic needs are met, time itself matters so much more.

Mostly Es—Explorer

There's no adventure your little one won't take, no butterfly she won't follow, no sprinkler she doesn't run through. She prefers to spend her days immersing herself in new experiences, and has the physical endurance of a child three times her age. Sometimes her wandering tendencies can be a bit exhausting, but if you pack enough food and water, you'll start to love life as a road trip, even if the road is just the sidewalk and the trip is just across the yard.

Brain Boosters

Here are a few tried-and-tested techniques to pique your toddler's curiosity and improve her behavior—and make you look like a super-parent while you're at it!

- Make time for lots of exercise. If your little tot is racing around the house, jumping where she's not supposed to jump, swinging where she's not supposed to swing—she *probably* needs more time running around outside.

- Get outside, no matter the weather. Kids love rain, and besides the obvious puddle-jumping and summer-bathing-suit-rain-shower-run, you can always add some science to the mix. Try measuring the rainfall in a bucket or leaving a drawing outside and seeing what happens.

- Play "I Spy" as you're taking a walk and ask your child to find the color, shape, or number you're "spying." Don't shy away from advanced shapes, pointing to the crescent moon or explaining that a stop sign is an octagon. You'll be surprised what your toddler will pick up.

- Talk to your toddler, even if it's just running through your shopping list together. You'll never have a better audience!

- Ask your child for alternate endings to familiar stories. Ask "what if" questions that will change the plot in entertaining ways.

- Don't shy away from using big words. More often than not your child will absorb the word based on context (as he does for all the little words you use every day). Remember those things called dictionaries? Keep yours within reach and try to pick a new word of the day every day. Why not learn with your toddler?

- Bring up math whenever you can, in fun and simple ways. When you're cutting up a pizza, ask: How many slices do I have? What fraction of the whole is this piece? Don't worry about mastery at this stage—as with new vocabulary, just focus on exposure.

- Discuss the latest scientific discoveries—it's so much fun to get a toddler's take. "People might go live on Mars soon!" you say breathlessly one morning, reading about NASA's latest mission. "Why wouldn't they?" answers your toddler. In toddler-world, anything's possible, which is the upside we have to remember when we're exhausted, frustrated, and covered in goop.

- Carry a pocket book of poems with you, and whenever you're waiting for a bus, or in a doctor's office, or in a restaurant, break it out and read a few to your child. They love nonsense rhymes, especially limericks.

Conclusion

This book follows *Test Your Baby's IQ,* and they both follow *Test Your Dog's IQ.* I had a dog before I had a baby, so you could say *I* was tested by my dog before I was tested by a baby or toddler. But the number of similarities between all three is rather surprising. They're hard to confine, take lots of naps, and routinely eat off the floor.

It's when it comes to misbehavior that I feel the most compelled to repeat my caveat from the dog books, to say that noncompliance on a test, or even when it comes to overall comportment, is often interpreted as a sign of ineptitude. It's not. A dog who doesn't come when called or a child who doesn't fill in the correct bubble on a test might both be judged as less intellectually promising than their more responsive peers, but perhaps it's some elusive alchemy of creative defiance that keeps them from performing "well." As the cliché for the rebel artist now goes, they may prefer to "draw outside the lines." Except in rare cases, society does not reward outside-the-line-drawers—it prefers followers, well-trained dogs and people. (As a little light bedtime reading, try Sigmund Freud's *Civilization and Its Discontents.*)

This book does not attempt to measure intelligence—as vastly complicated and controversial a task as that is, even for canines—but rather to help you assess your toddler's particular strengths and interests. The questions are supposed to be light-hearted, and the activities fun and hopefully good for a laugh. You certainly don't need to invent an obstacle course for your little stuntman or stuntwoman—each day in your life together presents enough challenges as it is.

But soon enough you'll realize, with a toddler leading the way, every detour can lead you to something wonderful— even if it's just watching as he examines a worm for the first time, and makes you laugh as he points to it and calls it a "snake." You'll start to truly understand the Zen saying, "The obstacle is the path." Maybe you'll even change your pace to adapt to your toddler's, change your course to follow his path, rather than the other way around.

Just as all children are naturally inquisitive, they're naturally inventive, too. The best thing we can do is keep encouraging them to ask questions, reminding them what the man whose name is synonymous with genius once said:

"To raise new questions, new possibilities, to regard old problems from a new angle requires creative imagination and marks real advance in science."

—Albert Einstein

Bibliography

Ames, Louise Bates and Frances L. ILG, M.D., *Your Three-Year-Old: Friend or Enemy*, Dell, 1980

Fraiberg, Selma, *The Magic Years: Understanding and Handling the Problems of Early Childhood*, Scribner 1996

Gardner, Howard E., *Multiple Intelligences: New Horizons in Theory and Practice*, Basic Books, 2006

Klein, Tovah P., *How Toddlers Thrive: What Parents Can Do Today for Children Ages 2-5 to Plant the Seeds of Lifelong Success*, Touchstone, 2014

Krueger, Caryl, *1,444 Fun Things to Do With Kids: Creative, Wholesome, and Educational Activities for Families*. Tess Press, 2009

Ruf, Deborah L., "How smart is my child?" *New York Parenting*, 2010. Web, June 2016

ACKNOWLEDGMENTS

I'm grateful to Hazel Eriksson and Helen Rochester for their deft editing of the manuscript and to Ellen Crenshaw once again for her delightful illustrations. Thanks Wally and Petra for always asking questions.